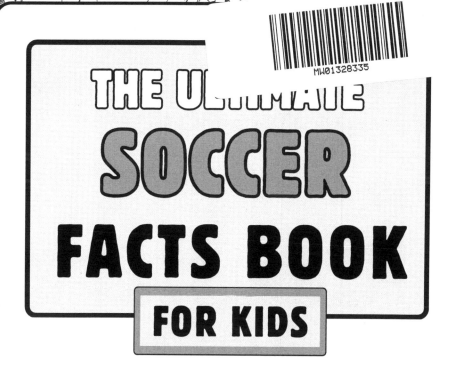

Broadwood Press are an independent publishing team that aims to provide fun and educational books for young readers.

All facts within this book are accurate at the time of publishing. However, if you happen to spot anything that needs to be corrected, please email us at **broadwoodpress@gmail.com** and we will be more than happy to help you out.

ISBN: 9798303695924

Copyright © 2024 by Broadwood Press

All rights reserved.

No portion of this book may be reproduced in any form without written permission from the publisher or author.

1.

The first form of soccer originated in China in 3 BC.

2.

During that time, the Chinese called the game 'Cuju'.

3.

Brazil has won more World Cups (five) than any other country.

4.

Germany and Italy closely follow them on four wins.

5.

The first-ever World Cup was hosted in Uruguay in 1930.

6.

Surprisingly, Uruguay won the tournament, which is their only World Cup title to date.

7.

Germany has reached more World Cup finals than any other country (eight).

8.

Brazil are the only country to play in every single World Cup.

9.
Formed in 1857, Sheffield FC is considered the first official soccer club.

10.
MLS (Major League Soccer) was founded in 1993.

11.
However, the first MLS season wasn't until 1996.

12.
Chris Wondolowski holds the MLS record for most goals scored (171 goals).

13.
FIFA stands for 'Federation Internationale de Football Association'.

14.
FIFA was founded in Paris in 1904.

15.
The World Cup has been decided by a penalty shootout on three occasions (1994, 2006 and 2022).

16.
Real Madrid are the only team to have won the Champions League more than ten times.

17.
Zinedine Zidane was named FIFA World Player of the Year three times in his career.

18.
He won the award in 1998, 2000 and 2003.

19.
Nigeria has won the U17 World Cup more times than any other country (five).

20.
The first Women's World Cup was held in China in 1991.

21.
Manchester United was founded in 1878 as 'Newton Heath LYR Football Club'.

22.
Cristiano Ronaldo has won five Ballon d'Or awards in his career and has scored over 700 goals.

23.
More than 1.1 million fans attended the 2019 Women's World Cup.

24.
Hungary beat Germany 8-3 in the 1954 World Cup.

25.
The first soccer match to be televised was between Arsenal and Arsenal Reserves in 1937.

26.
The term 'Soccer' was actually first created by the English in the late 1800s.

27.
Pele scored over 1,200 goals during his career.

28.
He also won three World Cup titles with Brazil.

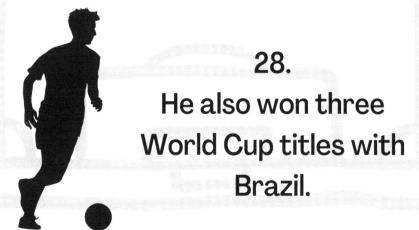

29.
Arsenal Women are the most successful English women's soccer club.

30.
The Ancient Greeks played a game similar to soccer called 'Episkyros'.

31.
Only thirteen teams participated in the first-ever World Cup.

32.
Cristiano Ronaldo won his first Ballon d'Or in 2008.

33.
Despite being one of the best nations at soccer, Spain has only won the World Cup once.

34.
Chelsea FC was founded in 1905.

35.
In 2017, Neymar moved from Barcelona to Paris Saint Germain for a record €222 million.

36.
Jose Mourinho has won more than twenty major trophies as a manager.

37.
The World Cup trophy is made from eighteen-carat gold.

38.
It also weighs 6.1 kilograms (16.6 lbs).

39.
The rivalry between AC Milan and Inter Milan is known as the 'Derby della Madonnina.'

40.
In 1314, the Lord Mayor of London banned soccer for causing 'chaos' in the city.

41.

Italy's Dino Zoff is the oldest player to win the World Cup.

42.

He won the 1982 World Cup at the age of 40.

43.

The first soccer-themed movie was the 1898 silent film 'Soccer Match'.

44.

Toronto FC became the first Canadian team to win the MLS cup (2017).

45.
Former Wigan player Manor Figueroa, only has three toes on his left foot.

46.
Rungrado 1st of May Stadium in North Korea is the largest soccer stadium in the world.

47.
The Tottenham Hotspur Stadium cost around $1.2 billion to build.

48.
The first soccer match to be televised in colour was between Liverpool and West Ham in 1969.

49.
Bob Paisley won three European Cups and six English League Titles as manager of Liverpool.

50.
The rivalry between Real Madrid and Barcelona is known as 'El Classico'.

51.
Pele was just 17 when he won the 1982 World Cup.

52.
Lionel Messi scored over 700 goals for Barcelona.

53.
The Copa Libertadores is the largest club competition in South America.

54.
The Copa Libertadores trophy is made from silver and weighs nine kilograms (20 lbs).

55.
Sir Matt Busby led Manchester United to their first European Cup in 1968.

56.
John Terry has scored the most Premier League goals as a defender (41).

57.
Stanley Matthews is the oldest player to win the Ballon d'Or (41 years old).

58.
Over 380 million people watched the 2021 Champions League final.

59.
Before 1912, goalkeepers were allowed to pick up the ball from anywhere on the pitch.

60.
No defender has scored more La Liga goals than Sergio Ramos (74).

61.
The Scottish FA Challenge Cup is the oldest soccer competition still being played.

62.
Adidas invented interchangeable screw-in studs on boots in the 1950s.

63.
The European Cup Winners' Cup was abolished in 1999.

64.
Eric Cantona moved to Man United for $2 million in 1992.

65.
It wasn't until the 1860s that the goalkeeper was officially introduced as a position in soccer.

66.
The Champions League trophy weighs 7.5 kilograms (16.5 lbs).

67.
Brazil's Marta has won six FIFA Women's World Player of the Year awards.

68.
Camp Nou, Spain, is the largest stadium in Europe (99,354 capacity).

69.
China's national team nickname is 'Zhong Guo Dui'.

70.
This translates to 'Team Dragon' in Chinese.

71.
Arsene Wenger has a degree in economics.

72.
The 1954 World Cup was the first to be broadcast on TV.

73.

Goalkeeper Rogerio Ceni scored 21 goals in the 2005 season.

74.

Iran's Ali Daei scored 109 goals in his career as a defender.

75.

Real Madrid won the first Champions League on the 13th June 1956.

76.

The Ballon d'Or trophy weights 2.5 kilograms (5.5 lbs).

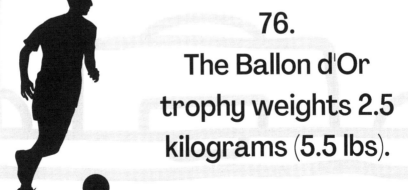

77.

NASA rejected Neil Armstrong's proposal to take a soccer ball to the moon for being too 'un-American'.

78.

The UEFA Champions League anthem was created by Tony Britten in 1992.

79.

Manchester United have won 20 Premier League titles, more than any other club.

80.

Eric Wynalda scored the first-ever MLS goal on April 6, 1996.

81.
Believe it or not, Hungary used to be one of the best national teams in the world.

82.
The Football Association (FA) was formed in 1863.

83.
The World Cup trophy was designed by an Italian artist named Silvio Gazzaniga.

84.
In 2021, the total value of the global soccer market was estimated to be over $75 billion.

85.
The 1994 World Cup Was hosted by the United States.

86.
Dani Alves won 43 major titles during his career.

87.
Clubs from Japan have won more AFC Champions League titles than any other country.

88.
Real Madrid is the most expensive soccer club in the world.

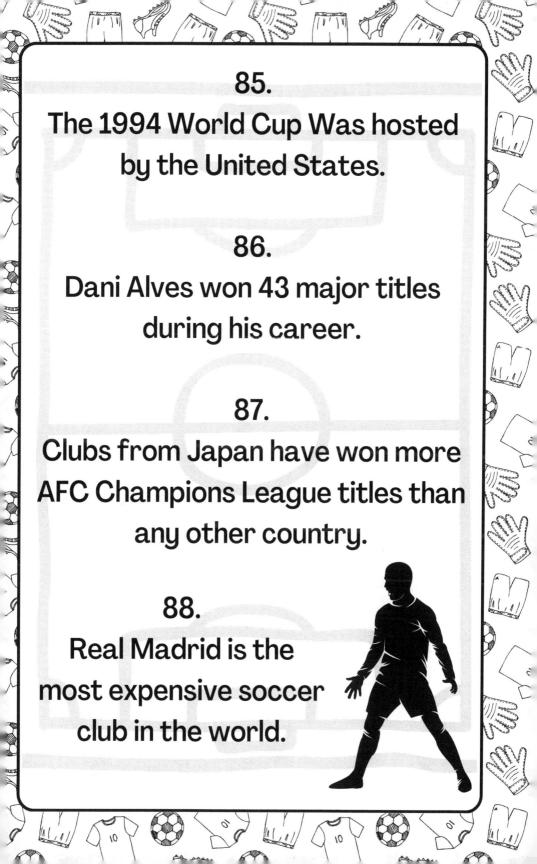

89.
The International Football Association Board (IFAB) determine the laws of soccer.

90.
'He Banged The Leather For Goal' was one of the first-ever soccer chants in England.

91.
Nike supplies 35% of the world's soccer kits.

92.
Iceland's national team nickname is 'Strakamir Okkar', meaning 'Our Boys' in Icelandic.

93.
Zlatan Ibrahimovic was the first player to score in every single minute of a soccer game.

94.
Cristiano Ronaldo is the only other player to have achieved this.

95.
René Higuita once performed a scorpion kick save during a match against England in 1995.

96.
England were the first team to win the World Cup wearing red.

97.
In 2019, Megan Rapinoe won both the Ballon d'Or and FIFA Women's World Player of the Year.

98.
Real Madrid's shirt sponsorship with Emirates is the most expensive in soccer history.

99.
The deal is an estimated $80 million per year.

100.
Cristiano Ronaldo has received at least one Ballon d'Or vote every year since 2003.

101.
In 1946, Stockport County and Doncaster Rovers played out a game that lasted three days.

102.
The first petition for VAR was started by the 'Royal Dutch Football Association' (KNVB) in 2014.

103.
In 1965, Keith Peacock became the first substitute in English soccer.

104.
Thierry Henry is Arsenal's all-time leading goalscorer.

105.
VAR was first trialled in a friendly between PSV and FC Eindhoven in 2016.

106.
In 2002, AS Adema beat Stade Olympique de L'Emyrne 149-0.

107.
Estadio Guillermo Plazas Alcid is the smallest stadium ever used during a World Cup.

108.
The Colombian stadium only had 8,000 seats at the time.

109.
The first-ever Copa Libertadores took place in 1960.

110.
More than 25 teams have won the tournament since.

111.
The IFAB officially approved the use of VAR in 2016.

112.
It's first official use came during the 2017 Confederations Cup.

113.
Chelsea are the only club to have held the Champions League and Europa League title at the same time.

114.
The lights outside The Allianz Arena (Munich) change colour to match the home team's colours.

115.
Women's soccer was first played the Olympics in 1996.

116.
Since 1982, every World Cup has included at least one Bayern Munich player.

117.
According to a French survey in 2018, around 13% of soccer watchers were against VAR.

118.
In 1966, the World Cup trophy was stolen but later found by a dog called Pickles.

119.
In 2015, Jamie Vardy scored in 11 consecutive Premier League matches.

120.
This is the record for the most consecutive Premier League games scored in.

121.
Gianfranco Zola is the only player to have been sent off in a World Cup on his birthday.

122.
Portsmouth's 7-4 win against Reading (2007) is the highest-scoring Premier League game ever.

123.
Lionel Messi has the most appearances for Barcelona (778).

124.
Giuseppe Bergomi has played in four World Cups, but never in a qualifying game.

125.
Nemanja Vidic is the only Premier League winner with a name made up of Roman Numerals.

126.
The highest scoring draw in Premier League history is 5-5.

127.
This classic was played out in 2013 between West Brom and Manchester United.

128.
It was also Sir Alex Ferguson's 1,500th and final game as United manager.

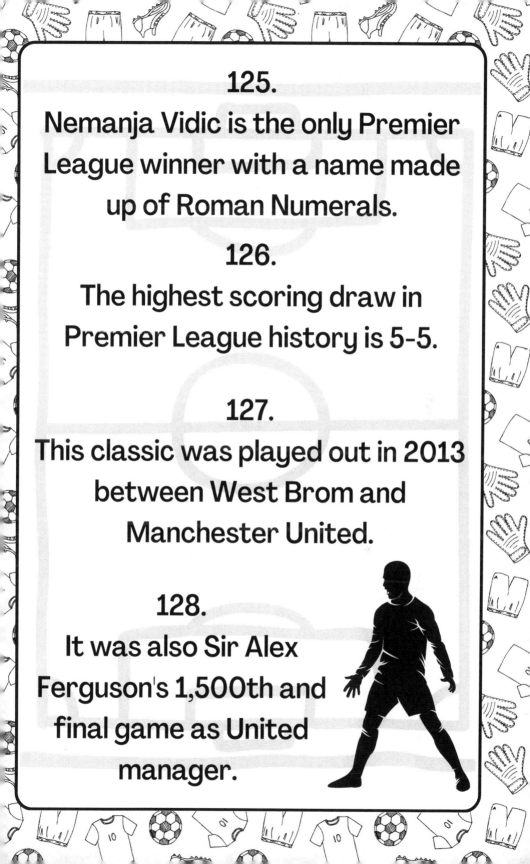

129.
Ryan Giggs holds the record for most appearances for Manchester United (632).

130.
Giggs also holds the Premier League appearance record.

131.
In the 2008/09 season, Edwin van der Sar went 1,300 minutes without conceding in the league.

132.
According to the IFAB, VAR is only used in 31% of games it's available in.

133.
Gary Lineker was never booked during his career.

134.
In 2023, Ilkay Gundogan scored the fastest goal in FA Cup final history.

135.
He scored after just 13 seconds in Manchester City's 2-1 win over rivals Manchester United.

136.
Petr Cech holds the record for most Premier League shutouts (202).

137.
The Maracana is the largest soccer stadium in Brazil.

138.
The old Arsenal badge had three canons sticking out the top of three lion heads.

139.
In 2001, Australian, Archie Thompson scored 13 goals in a single game.

140.
The goals came in Australia's 31-0 win against American Samoa.

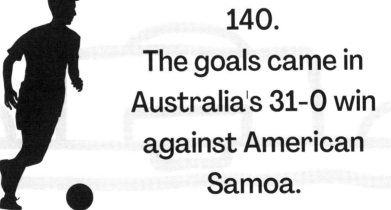

141.
Gerardo Bedoya received 46 red cards during his career.

142.
Alex Stepney dislocated his jaw whilst shouting at his defenders in 1975.

143.
Lionel Messi won his first Ballon d'Or in 2009.

144.
The first-ever Match of the Day game shown was between Liverpool and Arsenal in 1964.

145.
Cristiano Ronaldo's son is also called Cristiano.

146.
FC Barcelona players have more Ballon d'Or wins than any other club in the world.

147.
In May 2015, Sadio Mane scored the fastest hat trick in Premier League history.

148.
He scored the three goals in just 2 minutes and 56 seconds.

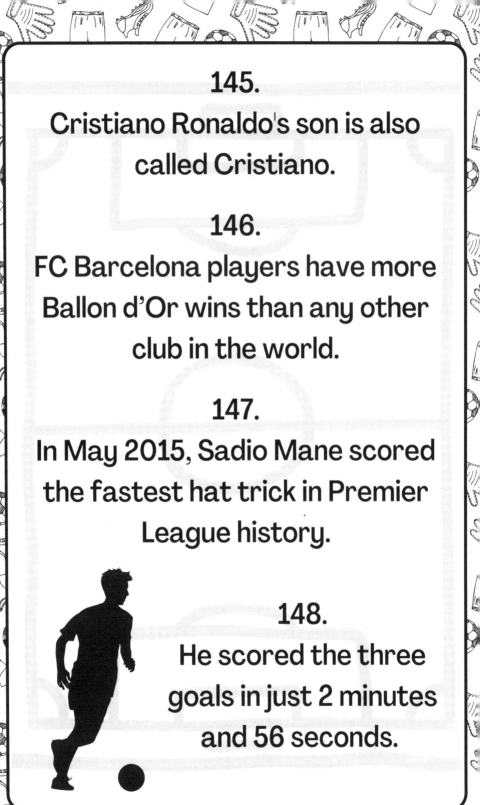

149.
Manchester United legend Sir Matt Busby played for Manchester City and Liverpool as a player.

150.
Peter Osgood's ashes are buried under the penalty spot at the Shed end of Stamford Bridge.

151.
98.9% of Ruud van Nistelrooy's Premier League goals were scored inside the box.

152.
In 2010/11, the most common first names in the Premier League were David and James.

153.
Moritz Volz scored the 15,000th Premier League goal, giving him the nickname '15,000 Volz'.

154.
Ryan Giggs was never sent off for Manchester United.

155.
In the 1904 Olympics, the U.S. men's team won both the silver and bronze medals in soccer.

156.
Juventus' nickname is 'The Old Lady'.

157.
Fulham vs Manchester United (2003) was the last Premier League game to not use a substitute.

158.
Jari Litmanen played international soccer over four separate decades.

159.
When Sweden play against Denmark, the scoreboard says SWE - DEN.

160.
The remaining letters then spell DEN-MARK.

161.
The lion on Chelsea's badge is copied from the coat of arms of an estate in Chelsea.

162.
Fitz Hall once acted in the movie 'The Fifth Element'.

163.
Before becoming a manager, Roy Hodgson was an English and PE teacher.

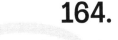

164.
Patrick Kluivert and Ruud van Nistelrooy are both born on the same day (July 1st, 1976).

165.
Every player in Shinji Kagawa's first international game in 2008 still played professional soccer 10 years later.

166.
Due to WWII, Portsmouth held the FA Cup title for seven years after 1939.

167.
John Obi-Mikel's name was spelt wrong during his registration process in 2003.

168.
It was incorrectly spelt, 'John Obi-Michael'.

169.
George Raynor was the first Englishman to manage in a World Cup final.

170.
In 2009 and 2010, Samuel Eto'o won consecutive trebles with Barcelona and Inter Milan.

171.
Between 1970 and 2018, Coventry City did not finish in the top six of any division.

172.
Hull City is the only team in the Football League with a name that has no closed letters.

173.
In 1987, Mark Hughes played for Wales and Bayern Munich on the same day.

174.
Messi led Argentina to the World Cup final in his first year as captain.

175.
Arsenal moved from Highbury to The Emirates Stadium in 2006.

176.
Norway has never lost a match against Brazil.

177.
The Arsenal captain used to be able to choose the length of the whole team's sleeves for a match.

178.
Manchester United won the first-ever Premier League in 1992-1993.

179.
Father and son Eidur and Arnor Gudjohnson both played in the same match in 1996.

180.
In 1908, Arsenal almost merged with Chelsea, Fulham, and Tottenham.

181.
Luka Modric and Mark Viduka are cousins.

182.
DC United won the first-ever MLS cup in 1996.

183.
Robert Earnshaw has scored a hat-trick in all levels of the Football League, the FA Cup, the League Cup and the Premier League.

184.
He's the only player in history to achieve this feat.

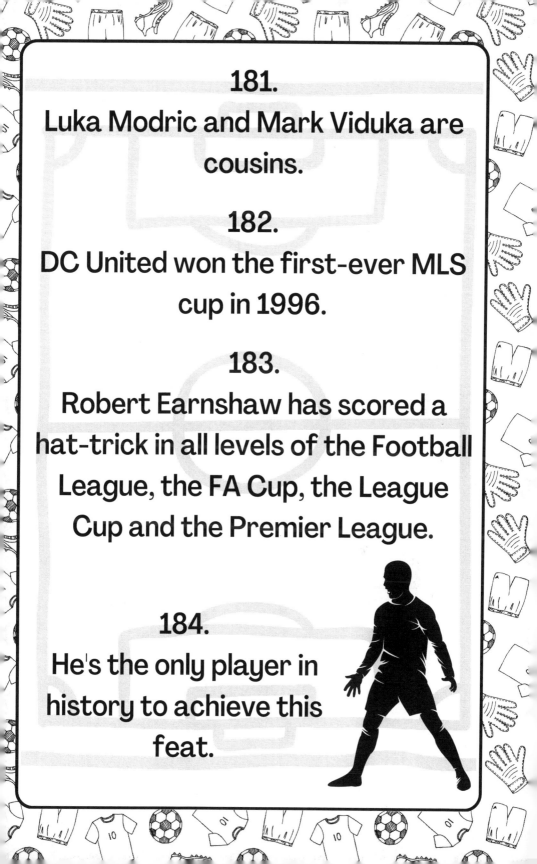

185.
Franz Beckenbauer threatened to move Bayern Munich to Italy in 2003.

186.
This resulted from the Bundesliga threatening Bayern with a points deduction following a controversial marketing deal.

187.
Jorginho was born in Brazil.

188.
The first 50 Premier League goals scored by a Bosnian were all scored by Edin Dezko.

189.
Alvin Martin once scored a hat-trick against three different goalkeepers.

190.
Marcus Rashford has helped give 21 million meals to children who cannot afford to eat.

191.
Rio Mavuba was born on a boat in international waters.

192.
Richard Dunne has scored the most Premier League own goals (10).

193.
Nick Ramando holds the MLS record for most shutouts (154).

194.
He also holds the record for the most MLS games played (514).

195.
Landon Donovan holds the record for the most MLS assists (136).

196.
In 2012, Lionel Messi scored 91 goals in a single year.

197.
Gary Lineker famously introduced Match of the Day in his underwear after Leicester City won the Premier League.

198.
Over 300 million people worldwide are officially registered to play soccer in some form.

199.
Cameroon beat Argentina in 1990 with only nine players.

200.
Juninho Pernambucano scored 77 free kicks in his career.

201.
An inflated pig's bladder was used as a soccer ball in ancient times.

202.
Ravshan Irmatov has refereed more World Cup games than any other referee (11).

203.
Paolo Di Canio was once fined $12,500 for pushing a referee.

204.
In DR Congo in 1998, lighting strikes killed an entire soccer team.

205.
Pele was the first to refer to soccer as 'the beautiful game'.

206.
Ryan Giggs has been substituted more than any other Premier League player.

207.
Despite playing against them four times, Dundee United have never lost a game against Barcelona.

208.
Over half the world's population watched the 2022 World Cup.

209.
In 1971, Groningen only conceded seven goals during an entire season.

210.
Mike Dean has refereed more Premier League games than any other ref.

211.
The Ancient Romans used to play a version of soccer called 'Harpastum'.

212.
In 2012, UEFA banned Malaga for four seasons for failing to pay taxes and wages.

213.
Owen Hargreaves is the only player to have played for England before living in the UK.

214.
Australia didn't lose a single game during their 1998 World Cup qualifying campaign.

215.
Shockingly, they still failed to qualify for the tournament.

216.
AC Milan won the Serie A in 1993/94 despite only scoring 36 goals.

217.
Cristiano Ronaldo has scored more of his goals in the 23rd minute than in any other.

218.
FC Barcelona have built 16,000 schools in countries around the world.

219.
Valdemar de Brito was the first player to miss a penalty kick in the World Cup.

220.
Salomon Rondon scored a hat-trick of headers in 2016.

221.
Bringing celery into Stamford Bridge is banned.

222.
This is because fans used to bring it into the stadium to throw onto the pitch.

223.
Andres Iniesta scored fewer La Liga goals for Barcelona than John Terry scored Premier League goals for Chelsea.

224.
Soccer balls were used in the first-ever games of basketball.

225.
Johan Cruyff won four Ballon d'Or awards as a player.

226.
Giorgio Chiellini has a Master's Degree in Business Administration.

227.
Simon Mignolet can speak five different languages.

228.
David Beckham was the first player to be sent off twice for England.

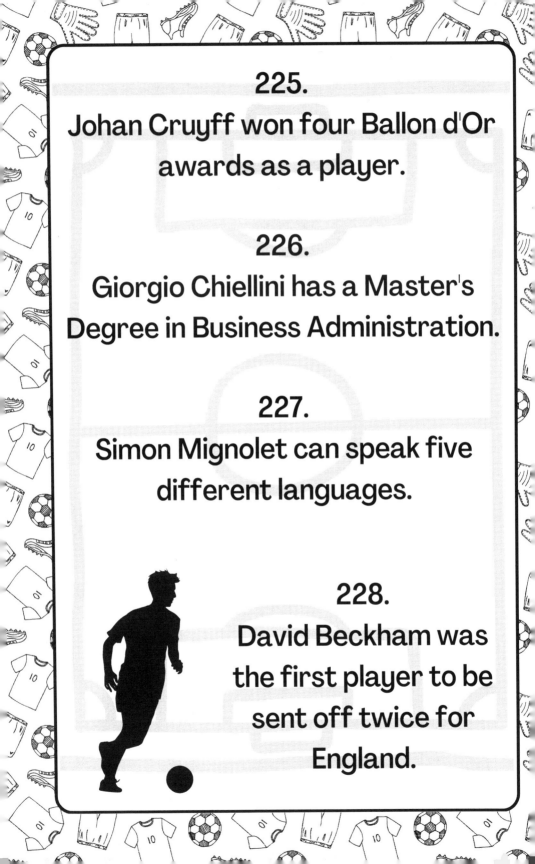

229.
In 1989, Fernando d'Ercoli ate a red card that was given to him.

230.
Manuel Neuer was a voice actor in the German version of 'Monsters University'.

231.
Aberdeen was the last club to beat Real Madrid in a European Cup final (1983).

232.
David Beckham once scored from the halfway line wearing someone else's boots.

233.
Former Arsenal player Alex Song has 27 siblings.

234.
The MLS averages over 22,000 spectators every game.

235.
The World Cup trophy spent WWII in a shoe box under Ottorino Baressi's bed in Italy.

236.
There is an asteroid named after Arsene Wegner.

237.
Mike Bagley once took a referee's notebook, ripped out the page with his name on it, and ate it.

238.
The average professional soccer player runs 10km during a game.

239.
Gary and Phil Neville's father was called Neville Neville.

240.
Javier Zanetti played over 500 Serie A matches before he was sent off.

241.
Due to his fear of airplanes, Dennis Bergkamp was known as the 'Non-Flying Dutchman'.

242.
According to FIFA, 29 million women play soccer every year.

243.
Rio Ferdinand was never picked in a European Championship squad but was named in four World Cup squads.

244.
Angel Di Maria was once bought in exchange for 35 soccer balls.

245.
Gareth Bale is the only British soccer player to win the Champions League five times.

246.
The size of a soccer ball hasn't changed in 120 years.

247.
Steaua Bucharest once went on a 106-game unbeaten streak.

248.
Over 60% of the world's soccer balls are made in Pakistan.

249.
The 'National Football Museum' was moved to Manchester in 2012.

250.
Many MLS games are played on artificial turf which increases the chances of injury.

251.
FC Barcelona's club motto is 'Mes Que un Club', which translates to 'more than a club' in English.

252.
India withdrew from the 1950 World Cup because they weren't allowed to play barefoot.

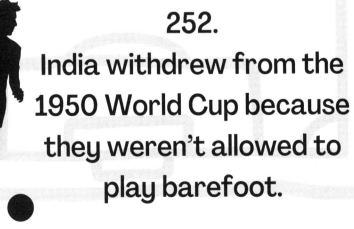

253.
The first international game of soccer took place in 1872 between Scotland and England.

254.
New Zealand were the only undefeated team in the 2010 World Cup.

255.
Fernando Torres captained Atletico Madrid while Diego Simeone still played there.

256.
In 2014, three Chelsea goalkeepers were awarded a shutout in the same game.

257.
David Moyes and David Beckham have played in the same team.

258.
They were in the same Preston team in the 1994/1995 season.

259.
Despite being from Austria, Rapid Vienna has won a German Bundesliga title.

260.
This means they have more Bundesliga titles than Shalke.

261.
Javier Mascherano's first match in senior soccer was for the Argentina national team.

262.
A coin toss decided the 1968 European Championship semi-final.

263.
Ferenc Puskas played for Spain in the 1962 World Cup.

264.
There was no final at the 1950 World Cup.

265.
In this World Cup, the final four teams were put into a small group to decide the winner.

266.
Johan Cruyff once played for PSG.

267.
Aston Villa were more successful than Manchester United before Sir Alex Ferguson took charge.

268.
Feyenoord goalkeeper Ronald Graafland had to wait 18 years to make his debut for the team.

269.
Bobby Zamora has scored a Premier League penalty with both his left and right foot.

270.
France were awarded the first-ever penalty by VAR, in 2018.

271.
They also had the first-ever goal dissalowed by VAR in 2017.

272.
In 2014, Karim Benzema scored the first-ever goal awarded by goal-line technology.

273.
Owen Hargreaves played for Wales at U19 level.

274.
The Brunei national team won the Malaysian Cup in 1999.

275.
Ironically, David Beckham was born at a hospital called 'Whipps Cross'.

276.
More than half of France's ten most capped players played in the Euro 2000 final.

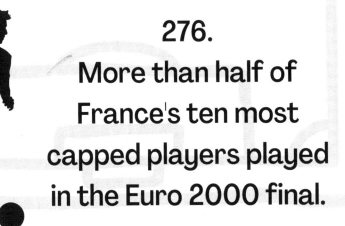

277.
Hans-Jorg Butt (a goalkeeper) has scored three champions league goals.

278.
All three of his goals were penalties and were scored against Juventus.

279.
The United States Soccer Federation (USSF) is the governing body for the MLS.

280.
Nottingham Forest has won more European Championships than English Championships.

281.
Boca Juniors stole their kit colours from the Swedish national team.

282.
Dejan Stankovic has played for three different national teams at World Cups.

283.
Clarence Seedorf has won the Champions League with three different teams.

284.
He won it with Ajax in 1995, Real Madrid in 2000, and AC Milan in 2003 and 2007.

285.
Arsenal are the only team to go unbeaten for a whole Premier League season.

286.
They are also one of the few teams to have never been relegated.

287.
Motherwell won the Copa del Rey in 1927.

288.
Swansea City are the only other non-Spanish team to have played in the competition.

289.
James Milner made his Premier League debut before Harvey Elliot was born.

290.
The two then played alongside each other in the 2021/22 season.

291.
Harry Kane and Jamie Vardy both played in the same Leicester City team.

292.
Robert Prosinecki has scored for two different countries at a World Cup.

293.
He scored for Yugoslavia in 1990 and then Croatia in 1998.

294.
In 1994, Oleg Salenko won the World Cup Golden Boot despite not making it past the group stage.

295.
Guiseppe Bergomi never played in a World Cup qualifier despite getting 81 caps for Italy.

296.
In 1988, Ricardo Olivera scored after just 2.8 seconds for Uruguay.

297.
The Brazilian Ronaldo never won the Champions League.

298.
Charlie Adam is younger than Cristiano Ronaldo.

299.
Columbus Crew were the first MLS team to be founded.

300.
Ronaldinho once scored 23 goals in a single match for his youth team.

THE ULTIMATE SOCCER FACT BOOK

Broadwood Press

We hope you loved reading this book as much as we loved making it!!

If you enjoyed it as much as we hope, we'd love you to leave a review on Amazon and hear all about it!

We also have a range of other sports fact books on Amazon if you'd like to carry on the fun

Made in the USA
Middletown, DE
30 December 2024

68489916R00044